Theory Paper Grade 1   2016   A
Model Answers

1 (10)

(a)

(b)

2 *There are many ways of completing this question. The specimen completion below would receive full marks.* (10)

3 (10)

4 (10)

(a)   5th   2nd   1st /   6th   8th /   4th   7th   5th   3rd
              8th / 8ve   8ve / 1st

(b)

5 (10)

6 (10)

7 (10)

(a)

(b)　　　　D F♯ A　　　　　　G B D

8 (a)　at a walking pace / medium speed　(10)
100 crotchets in a minute / 100 quarter notes in a minute/
　　100 crotchet beats in a minute / 100 quarter-note beats in a minute
very quiet / very soft
accent / forced / accented
getting louder / gradually getting louder

(b)　(10)

　　(i)　semibreve / whole note
　　(ii)　6; 7
　　(iii)　　　　　　*legato* (smoothly)
　　(iv)　3 / 7
　　(v)　E

(c)　(10)

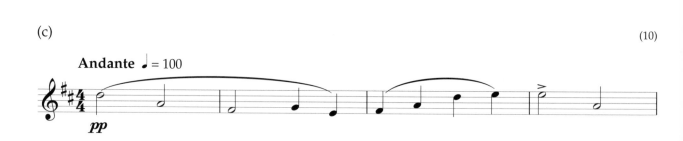

4

Grade

1

Music Theory Past Papers 2016

Model Answers

ABRSM Grade 1

Welcome to ABRSM's *Music Theory Past Papers 2016 Model Answers*, Grade 1. These answers are a useful resource for students and teachers preparing for ABRSM theory exams and should be used alongside the relevant published theory past papers.

All the answers in this booklet would receive full marks but not all possible answers have been included for practicable reasons. In these cases other reasonable alternatives may also be awarded full marks. For composition-style questions (where candidates must complete a rhythm, compose a melody based on a given opening or set text to music) only one example of the many possible answers is given.

For more information on how theory papers are marked and some general advice on taking theory exams, please refer to the Music Theory Grade 1 web page: www.abrsm.org/theory1.

Using these answers

- Answers are given in the same order and, where possible, in the same layout as in the exam papers, making it easy to match answer to question.

- Where it is necessary to show the answer on a stave, the original stave is printed in grey with the answer shown in black, for example:

- Alternative answers are separated by an oblique stroke (/) or by *or*, for example:

  getting slower / gradually getting slower

- The old-style crotchet rest is accepted as a valid alternative to the modern symbol .

- Answers that require the candidate to write out a scale or chord have been shown at one octave only. Reasonable alternatives at different octaves can also receive full marks.

- Sometimes the clef, key and time signature of the relevant bar(s) are included for added clarity, for example:

© 2017 by The Associated Board of the Royal Schools of Music
Published by ABRSM (Publishing) Ltd, a wholly owned subsidiary of ABRSM
Cover by Kate Benjamin & Andy Potts
Printed in England by Halstan & Co. Ltd, Amersham, Bucks, on materials from sustainable sources

Theory Paper Grade 1   2016   B
Model Answers

1   (10)

(a)

(b)

2 *There are many ways of completing this question. The specimen completion below would receive full marks.*   (10)

3   (10)

4   (10)

(a)   G   E   D   B   G   F#   C   A   F#

(b)   *There are two possible answers to this question. Either of the answers shown would receive full marks.*

5 (10)

6 (10)

7 (10)

8 (a) fast / quick / cheerful / lively (10)
crotchet beats / quarter-note beats
loud
very quiet / very soft
play the notes smoothly / slur

(b) (10)

(i) dotted minim / dotted half note
(ii) C / middle C
(iii) two
(iv) *There are three possible answers to this question. Any of the brackets shown would receive full marks.*

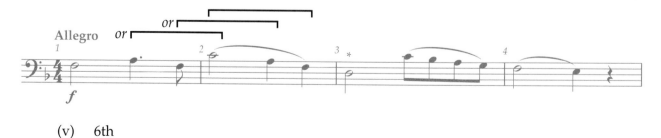

(v) 6th

(c)   (10)

Theory Paper Grade 1   2016   C
Model Answers

1   (10)

2 *There are many ways of completing this question. The specimen completion below would receive full marks.*   (10)

3   (10)

4   (10)

5   (10)

6   6th   3rd   4th   (10)
8th / 8ve   7th   5th

7   (10)

(a)   5th   4th   2nd   8th /   7th   6th   5th   3rd   1st /
                                   8ve / 1st   8th / 8ve

(b)   four

8   (a)   fast / quick / cheerful / lively   (10)
               the number of beats in a bar / two beats in a bar
               very loud
               play the notes detached / jumpy / staccato
               play the notes smoothly / slur

(b)   (10)

          (i)   quaver / eighth note
          (ii)   5
          (iii)

          (iv)   three
          (v)   G

(c)   (10)

Theory Paper Grade 1   2016   S
Model Answers

1 (10)

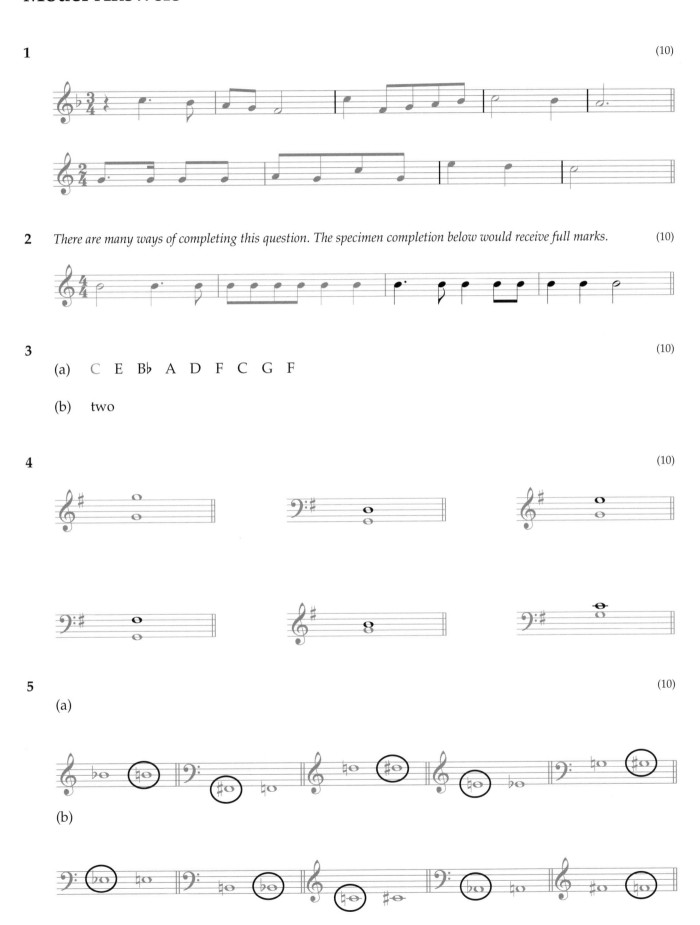

2 *There are many ways of completing this question. The specimen completion below would receive full marks.* (10)

3 (10)

(a)   C   E   B♭   A   D   F   C   G   F

(b)   two

4 (10)

5 (10)

(a)

(b)

(10)

7   G major   C major   D major
       C major   F major   D major

(10)

8   (a)   moderate speed / moderately
            moderately loud / half loud / medium loud
            getting louder / gradually getting louder
            accent / forced / accented
            getting slower / gradually getting slower

(10)

      (b)

(10)

            (i)   *There are five possible answers to this question. Any of the brackets shown would receive full marks.*

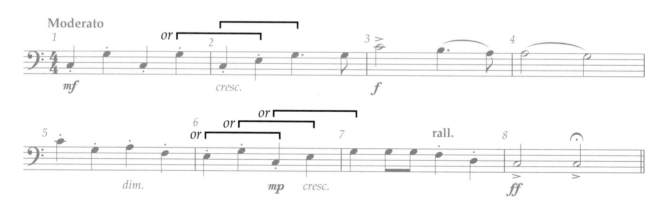

            (ii)   C / middle C
            (iii)   *staccato (detached)*
            (iv)   two
            (v)   8 / last bar

      (c)

(10)

Music Theory Past Papers 2016 Model Answers

Model answers for four past papers from ABRSM's 2016 Theory exams for Grade 1

Key features:

- a list of correct answers where appropriate
- a selection of likely options where the answer can be expressed in a variety of ways
- a single exemplar where a composition-style answer is required

Support material for ABRSM Music Theory exams

**Supporting the teaching and learning of music
in partnership with the Royal Schools of Music**

Royal Academy of Music | Royal College of Music
Royal Northern College of Music | Royal Conservatoire of Scotland

www.abrsm.org f facebook.com/abrsm
 @abrsm ABRSM YouTube

ISBN 978-1-84849-813-6